Lilies and Lemonade

Joy-filled Devotions

Written by Tracy Hill

ISBN: 978-0-9976913-1-3

Dedication

To Mom, a loving, kind, and beautiful woman, both inside and out. I'm so very blessed to call you my friend.

Introduction

Welcome to *Lilies and Lemonade*, a collection of whimsical stories, heartfelt devotions, and encouraging Scriptures. I like to think of it as a journey into Jesus-filled, joy-filled living. This little book is named according to two philosophies I try to govern my daily thinking by. The first is what I like to call *Lilies*, which the Bible uses to symbolize those who find their peace and rest as they regularly enter the Presence of God. Like the *lilies*, God encourages us to cease our endless striving and just be still, trusting in His tender care and ever-faithful provision. The second philosophy, which I've named *Lemonade*, comes from purposefully choosing an optimistic perspective, by looking for and discovering Jesus at work throughout our day. To me *lemonade* symbolizes taking the sour, tart events of life and turning them into something sweet and satisfying; it means looking at life through a glass half-filled mindset; it means turning my frown up-side down; looking for the brilliant silver lining in the dark and dreary clouds; and it most definitely involves counting my blessings and giving thanks to the LORD. Throughout this little book I hope to help you rest like the *lilies*, and think like *lemonade*. My purpose is to give you glimpses into both philosophies, and help you to find joy, hope, peace, optimism, and most importantly, Jesus in your daily life.

At the end of this book you will find blank journal pages which can be used to jot down notes, prayers, and thoughts that come to mind as you go through the devotions. The pages can also be used to write your own joy-filled stories of *Lilies and Lemonade*.

"And he said to his disciples, "Therefore I tell you, do not be anxious about your life, what you will eat, nor about your body, what you will put on. [23] For life is more than food, and the body more than clothing. [24] Consider the ravens: they neither sow nor reap, they have neither storehouse nor barn, and yet God feeds them. Of how much more value are you than the birds! [25] And which of you by being anxious can add a single hour to his span of life? [26] If then you are not able to do as small a thing as that, why are you anxious about the rest? [27] Consider the lilies, how they grow: they neither toil nor spin, yet I tell you, even Solomon in all his glory was not arrayed like one of these. [28] But if God so clothes the grass, which is alive in the field today, and tomorrow is thrown into the oven, how much more will he clothe you, O you of little faith! [29] And do not seek what you are to eat and what you are to drink, nor be worried. [30] For all the nations of the world seek after these things, and your Father knows that you need them. [31] Instead, seek his kingdom, and these things will be added to you.'" Luke 12:22-31 ESV

Great Gardens

We can find inspiration in the most random of ways. This morning my inspiration came through a nursery truck that was passing by. The words, *"Great Gardens Begin Here,"* were written across the side. It seems that was the claim and slogan for this local nursery. It occurred to me that this could also be the declaration for the Gospel message. "Great lives begin with Jesus." The gardens of our lives can be "great" when we allow God to be the Gardener— nurturing, nourishing, and pruning us to grow and flourish into an abundant display for His glory. The Gospel is the seed, our hearts are the soil, and the Word of God (Bible reading), praise, prayer, and fellowship are the water that is so vitally necessary for continual, healthy growth.

LORD, help my heart to be fertile soil. Let Your Word grow in my life and change me. May I blossom into a beautiful display of Your love, peace, hope, and joy. I pray that my life would be a reflection and testimony to the work of the Ultimate Gardener. In Jesus' name, Amen.

"But the seed falling on good soil refers to someone who hears the word and understands it. This is the one who produces a crop, yielding a hundred, sixty or thirty times what was sown."

Matthew 13:23

Blessed Interruptions

Early on a Saturday morning I was enjoying a time of Bible study. With my cup of coffee nearby and my workbook in hand, I was reflecting on the brevity of life described in the following verse—

"Show me, LORD, my life's end and the number of my days; let me know how fleeting my life is. You have made my days a mere handbreadth; the span of my years is as nothing before you. Everyone is but a breath, even those who seem secure." Psalm 39:4-5

I was reminded how short my time here is in the grand scheme of eternity. That time is fleeting and passes by oh, so quickly. I pondered this question: *How do I best spend this precious time?* Is it with the rigidity of sticking to an inflexible schedule, getting everything on my agenda done, avoiding any distractions and all interruptions?

This particular day I had sat down to do some quiet study; I had a purpose and a plan. As I was reflecting on this verse and what it means to me, my husband came up and said "Come with me, I want to show you something". Sometimes I get a little annoyed when I am interrupted right in the middle of something. But, I put down my study, got up from my seat and followed him upstairs, where he led me out onto the balcony. The view was amazing; the sky was crystal clear, and a warm breeze was blowing. As we stood there together enjoying the view, our ears perked up to the sound of the "Star Spangled Banner," being sung from the park nearby. As the song ended we heard the baseball crowd cheer and applaud. Just think, if I had stuck to my plan and not embraced the moment, I would have missed out on the spontaneous blessing I experienced with my loved one. I was truly blessed by being present in the moment, and embracing the interruption.

So often we miss out on the present (the gift of the moment), because we ourselves are not fully present; we are too busy and our minds are preoccupied. How often are we engaged in the action of texting, or checking our phones, or doing something else, while we should be enjoying the company of those in our actual presence? We cannot build relationships or create fulfilling memories when we are only half engaged. We must consciously decide to step into the moment and notice, appreciate, and savor every bit of it, always allowing room for blessed interruptions.

"Teach us how short life is, so that we may become wise."

Psalm 90:12

Lemonade

Let me share with you about the time I got a new car. Actually, it was better than new, it was used with very few miles on it—which meant we got a really good deal... or so we thought. I was enjoying this new car of mine. It was the perfect size; it was nice and roomy, with plenty of cargo space and better gas mileage than my previous car. Well, not long after our purchase it started breaking down. It got to the point where we had to call a tow truck about twice a week. They would tow it to the dealership, fix it up, and then call us to come pick it up. After a few days, the cycle would repeat. It seems the engine could not cool properly. The gauges revealed the engine over-heating, as fluid would pour out of the bottom. We knew we had a lemon, but we had to endure the process. Eventually the dealership would have to agree with us and officially declare it a lemon.

So, one day (when it was supposedly fixed) I took the boys and our cousin for a fun-filled day at the beach. On our drive home, we took the steepest and windiest canyon of all. We had made our way to the top of the canyon when suddenly the red lights began flashing and the check engine light began blaring. Smoke or steam (not sure which) started to come out from under the hood. We quickly pulled over and jumped out of the car. I knew my car might be lost, but I didn't want to have to replace beach chairs on top of that. So, we quickly got everything that wasn't nailed down out of the car and then moved a bit away. I called my husband, and he called the tow truck, *again*. Now, while we were waiting, we could have been stressed out, letting the joy of our beach day turn sour, but instead we chose to have a party of sorts. We unfolded our beach chairs, opened the cooler, got out some snacks and drinks. As we sat there relaxing (safely away from the car and the edge of the road), cars would drive by

4

periodically. We began smiling and waving *hello* to all the passerby's. Everyone would wave, smile, honk, and holler *hello* back, but no one ever stopped to see if we needed help. I suppose because of our joyful adaptation to our circumstances, we looked like we were purposefully having a great time hanging out on the side of the road. Eventually the tow truck did come, and eventually our car was declared a lemon. So, everything turned out just fine.

And that's my story of how to take a lemon and make lemonade—take a bad circumstance and turn it into an opportunity for an impromptu celebration.

Seeing things through God's perspective and looking for the joy in situations keeps us on our feet—impervious to defeat. A *lemonade* outlook keeps us from being side-tracked or knocked off balance when trials come.

The way we choose to handle difficult situations can positively benefit us, but it can also bring glory to God as we trust in Him.

Do I always react this well? Unfortunately, no. But it sure is nicer when I do.

"But may the righteous be glad and rejoice before God; may they be happy and joyful." Psalm 68:3

Desperately

God desperately loves us, but doesn't necessarily need us.

We desperately need God, but do we necessarily love Him?

I hope in the end we find that we desperately do.

"As the deer pants for streams of water, so my soul pants for you, my God." Psalm 42:1

Simplicity

I have concluded that simplicity begins with God. We are the ones who complicate things. We add unnecessary busyness into days that are already over-filled and over-flowing with burdensome distractions that keep us from enjoying the blessings God wants to fill our lives with. As we keep company with God though, He sets about changing our priorities. He properly orders our days; He begins to weed out the time stealers; He shows us what to say "yes" to, and what to say "no" to. As we walk in rhythm with Jesus and take on His plans for our lives, everything seems to fall into place. Everything is simplified. Exchange our schedule for His. Exchange our plans for His. Exchange our burdens for His. He invites us to make this exchange and simplify.

"Come to me, all you who are weary and burdened, and I will give you rest. [29] Take my yoke upon you and learn from me, for I am gentle and humble in heart, and you will find rest for your souls. [30] For my yoke is easy and my burden is light."

Matthew 11:28-30

Be You

You are amazing.

You are wonderful.

You are unique.

You are beautiful.

You are creative.

You are special.

You are important.

You are created by God.

Don't try to be anyone else.

Just be you!

"You are altogether beautiful, my darling; there is no flaw in you."

Song of Songs 4:7

Attitude of Lilies

A lily seeks God first and lets all else fall into place accordingly. A lily doesn't strive to be good enough, working hard to earn the Father's favor; a lily rests in the simplicity of the Gospel Message—that Jesus is enough on her behalf, and that she already has God's favor. A lily invests her life in treasures that will last; she strips away distractions and gets back to the basics in God's Presence. A lily experiences calm amid storms, by keeping her eyes on Jesus, by trusting completely in Him, allowing Him to replace her chaos with His peace. A lily makes time with Jesus a consistent priority; she doesn't just pop in for an occasional visit with Him, she abides and remains in Him. She stops, sits, listens, and rests at His feet for continual refreshment. A lily stands on the fundamental foundation of her salvation, which is found in her Savior, and she lives out her salvation daily with grace and love toward others. She doesn't complicate her relationship with Jesus by turning it into a religion of rules and regulations. She simply rests, and loves.

"Consider the lilies, how they grow: they neither toil nor spin, yet I tell you, even Solomon in all his glory was not arrayed like one of these." Luke 12:27

In Progress

Don't be too hard on yourself—you are a work in progress. God is patient with you. He knows you're still growing. He showers you with grace daily, and if God is willing to show you grace, then I'm sure He'd like for you to allow yourself some grace too. God is changing you, refining you, perfecting you, little by little, day by day. He's not finished with you yet; be patient, and remember you're a work in progress. God knows your struggles; He sees your weaknesses. He doesn't demand perfection today, but He knows you will be perfect someday. When Jesus comes back you will finally be made perfect—but not until then. God began the good work in you, and He is faithful to complete it. Take the pressure off yourself and just surrender to God. And let Him do the work of bringing you to perfection.

"In all my prayers for all of you, I always pray with joy [5] because of your partnership in the gospel from the first day until now, [6] being confident of this, that he who began a good work in you will carry it on to completion until the day of Christ Jesus." Philippians 1:4-6

Both Feet

Every day we are faced with decisions and opportunities—some big, some small. Nevertheless, there are choices to be made in one way or another. It is always best to assess, process and consider a matter before making a choice. When faced with any decision, I pray that the Lord would give me insight to what is most beneficial; that He would share His knowledge and wisdom with me. The best place to find wisdom is in pausing before His glorious throne for guidance and direction before venturing onward. As the LORD does reveal His wisdom to me and points me in the right direction, I then pray for the faith to act upon it— like that of a little child. I pray for a faith that eagerly grabs hold of Jesus' hand, runs to the water's edge, and jumps in whole-heartedly with both feet and without fear.

"But Jesus called the children to him and said, 'Let the little children come to me, and do not hinder them, for the kingdom of God belongs to such as these. ⁷Truly I tell you, anyone who will not receive the kingdom of God like a little child will never enter it.'"

Luke 18:16-17

Fully Submersed

For most folks, the summer season begins with Memorial Day Weekend. Summer is punctuated with fireworks on the Fourth of July, and is filled with the aroma of hamburgers and hot dogs.

As for me, I don't totally sense that summer has arrived until I have fully submersed myself in the waves of the ocean. Today was that day, the day that summer truly came alive for me. I set aside the afternoon and ventured to the beach with my lovely aunt. We were greeted by a bright blue sky, and sparkling turquoise waters, which formed into white rolling waves. The warm and grainy sand clung between my toes. The sun warmed my skin till the ocean called my name, and beckoned me to take a dip. On a beautiful day like this, a dip would never be enough. So, I go deeper. I love the feel of the waves washing completely over me, from the tip of my toes, to the top of my head. The cool, salty water surprises and refreshes me as I plunge completely in. The waves roll in one after another. I am filled with delight as wave after wave crashes over me, taking my breath away each time.

As I look at the waves, as I feel them crash over me, I am reminded of God's amazing love for me. There is even a popular song with lyrics describing the love of God in this manner that runs through my mind.

God's love is relentless, it is powerful, it refreshes my soul, it is endless, it makes me brave, and it takes my breath away.

Come into His Presence today and let Him wash you in His love.

"I pray that from his glorious, unlimited resources he will empower you with inner strength through his Spirit. [17] Then Christ will make his home in your hearts as you trust in him. Your roots will grow down into God's love and keep you strong. [18] And may you have the power to understand, as all God's people should, how wide, how long, how high, and how deep his love is. [19] May you experience the love of Christ, though it is too great to understand fully. Then you will be made complete with all the fullness of life and power that comes from God." Ephesians 3:16-21

Handful of Quietness

Turn off the noise. Be silent, in solitude. Easier said than done, but essential to our well-being. Our minds and bodies need a break from the constant *doing* we demand of them. There comes a time when we eventually run ourselves ragged to the place of exhaustion, and are of no good to anyone. Before we get to this breaking point let's purposefully allow ourselves time to reset, refresh, and reinvigorate in the quiet Presence of God. Our minds and bodies were designed to require time for just being still. Taking a break from all the doing, to enjoy some alone time with the LORD is a necessity, not a luxury. In these moments, we gather handfuls of quietness to carry our souls onward. Let's get in the practice of permitting ourselves these necessary times of just *being* in His Presence.

"Better is a handful of quietness than two hands full of toil and a striving after wind." Ecclesiastes 4:6 ESV

His Will

Grumbling robs God of His glory. Complaining cheats us of our joy. Endless griping can be downright wearisome. God instead asks us to turn our concerns over to His care where some good can truly be accomplished. Repeating our frustrations over and over is just plain unproductive. Offering our needs and worries into the capable hands of our LORD opens the door to His effective power. His will is that we continually bring our requests to Him, and that we do it joyfully, with thankful hearts and rejoicing mouths, regardless of our circumstances.

Let's drink from a glass half-full as we bring our requests to God. Let's be thankful and rejoice as we acknowledge His provisions and appreciate the blessings He pours out daily.

"Rejoice always, [17] pray continually, [18] give thanks in all

circumstances; for this is God's will for you in Christ Jesus."

1 Thessalonians 5:16-18

Uniquely Made

My lime green pants were a gift from my grandma. They were covered in little white daisies, with bright reds centers. For a time, they were my favorite. I wore them frequently enough, but If I'd had my way I'm sure I would have worn them every day. They were happy pants. They made me feel good, despite the fact they weren't the most fashionable. I wore them for me, not for anyone else. Isn't it sad that we lose this confidence as we grow—the confidence to be uniquely us—and feel the need to conform to someone else's idea of what is good and appropriate, in the process losing ourselves. God created us each in a special way. He made us each with distinct likes, dislikes, personalities, qualities, characteristics, and even quirks, which He would love for us celebrate. We bring honor to Him as we allow ourselves the freedom of being uniquely us, how He created us to be.

The following definitions are found on Merriam-Webster.com:

- **Individuality:** Total character peculiar to and distinguishing an individual from others; separate or distinct existence; individual; person

- **Originality:** the quality or state of being original; fresh of aspect, design or style; the power of independent thought or constructive imagination

"I praise you because I am fearfully and wonderfully made; your works are wonderful, I know that full well." Psalm 139:14

Let today be the day you confidently stand apart from the crowd, and allow yourself the freedom to be the individual and original version of *you*. Even if it involves lime green, flowered pants, be courageously and uniquely *you*.

In the Stillness

In the rush of the day we often lose our sense of God's Presence. It is in the quiet and stillness that our hearts and minds become more fully aware of Him. By stepping outside of the busyness— even for just a few moments—to spend quality, undistracted time with God, we reap untold blessings of peace, clarity, calm, and refreshment to carry us through the demands of the day. In the quiet and stillness, we find Him.

"He makes me lie down in green pastures, he leads me beside quiet waters," Psalm 23:2

Confidence

My confidence is found not in others' opinion of me; not in my assessment of myself; not in my looks, ability, possessions, position, wealth, or power. My confidence is found not even in my blessings. All of these can change in an instant like the direction of the wind. The one, sure, constant truth I find my confidence in is my identity as a daughter of the King and my position of royalty in God's kingdom. My confidence is found in my permanent place of belonging in my Father's household. My confidence is found in God alone.

"For the LORD will be your confidence and will keep your foot from being caught." Proverbs 3:26, ESV

Crowns of Celebration

Hats can say a lot about who we are and about our situation. Hard hats are worn by construction workers for protection as they enter building sites. Baseball hats are worn by players to shield their eyes from the sun, allowing them to spot the ball as it closes in. Train engineers are known by striped conductor's hats; cowboys are recognized by their wide-brimmed hats of straw or felt; chefs are distinguished by the tall white hats sitting upon their heads. Throughout the centuries hats have been worn as symbols of status and style. Hats are often worn for celebration, as when people don pointy, cone-shaped, paper hats decorated with colorful designs, to honor a birthday.

A special weekend with my mom and sister once turned into an extra-celebratory occasion as we decided our time together needed to be emphasized by wearing hats out on the town. We had each chosen a festive hat to commemorate our time together. These days, hat wearing isn't as prominent as in decades past, so everywhere we went people noticed and commented. We were surprised by the attention we received all because of the things that topped our heads. We were even asked what occasion prompted our hat-wearing. We replied that we were just celebrating our time together.

Even God has His hand in the hat business. His are called crowns though, and His will top our heads for all of eternity. His don't tarnish, bend, crumple, or wear out. God's are described as crowns of glory, crowns of salvation, honor, love and compassion, of victory, of eternal life and everlasting joy, of righteousness, and blessings. The crown He sets upon our heads will never fade away and will never be taken from us. Every day with the LORD calls for celebration and celebrations call for a crown. Our crowns speak volumes—they say loud and clear that we are a child of God, and they loudly proclaim of the rejoicing we have in His Presence.

"and those the LORD has rescued will return. They will enter Zion with singing; everlasting joy will crown their heads. Gladness and joy will overtake them, and sorrow and sighing will flee." Isaiah 35:10

Change

Change is inevitable for all of us. Change of residence, job, relationships, death, birth... Ecclesiastes 3:1-8 states that *there is a time and season for everything.* Nothing stays the same. From our vantage point, change often brings the opposite of peace. It brings uncertainty and chaos; it means letting go of the old and stepping out into the new. Change can be very hard even in the best of circumstances (I know for me it is). Our first response is to control everything; the process and the outcome. We like to think that if we can just keep control, everything will turn out okay. But peace is not found by keeping control; it's attained by surrendering control to the One who is ultimately in charge. And He is the One who will help us through the changes with His steady Presence.

The only way to maintain peace in our ever-changing lives is by keeping our eyes on Jesus.

Scripture assures us that God *"does not change like the shifting shadows."* James 1:17

"Jesus Christ is the same yesterday and today and forever." Hebrew 13:8

"Peace I leave with you; my peace I give you. I do not give to you as the world gives. Do not let your hearts be troubled and do not be afraid." John 14:27

The Wisest Way

"Now listen, you who say, 'Today or tomorrow we will go to this or that city, spend a year there, carry on business and make money.' ¹⁴ Why, you do not even know what will happen tomorrow. What is your life? You are a mist that appears for a little while and then vanishes. ¹⁵ Instead, you ought to say, 'If it is the Lord's will, we will live and do this or that.'" James 4:13-15

My days are not to be taken for granted. As much as I prepare and plan, I don't positively know what my future holds. As much as I'd like to tightly clutch the security of my life in my own hands, I know I can't. But how much more reassuring, to know that my life is in God's hands. I am not going to boast about my plans for today, tomorrow, or the distant future. I desire to know God's will for me. I won't be looking to the stars for guidance; I'll look to the Maker of the stars. He is the One who has given me this fresh new day, so I'm positive it would be a good idea to seek His wisdom and direction for it. How do I go about getting His wisdom? Just ask Him! Yes, it's that easy!

James 1:5 says, "if any of you lacks wisdom he should ask God, who gives generously to all..."

When we live by God's plans and wisdom we can get into bed at night knowing we lived this day in the *wisest way, His way.*

Child-like Faith

Remember when as a kid, in child-like faith you would climb aboard a friend's handlebars and fearlessly let them shuttle you around town? Your hands gripping the bars beneath you; your legs dangling freely, and a smile spread across your face. How time changes us. Now as an adult, in need of the feeling of control and calculation, we prefer to carefully climb aboard our own comfortable bicycle seat, steering ourselves in the direction of where we want to go. I once witnessed the potential perils of trusting someone else to control the bike while sitting upon the handlebars. Two teenage girls were joyfully riding along as they approached a stop light. They seemed to be going straight through the busy intersection despite the many cars around, when at the very last second the bicycle came to an abrupt halt, sending the handlebar rider flying off. Fortunately, she seemed unharmed as they were both laughing at the sudden event. It is precisely for this reason though, that we prefer to be in command of our own bicycle and rely on our own decision making. It feels like the safer choice and often this is true...with one major exception.

Jesus tells us to approach Him with trusting faith, like that of a child. The same wide-eyed abandon that once enabled us to climb aboard the handlebars, and the joy and laughter that ensued—this is what Jesus wants to share with us. He wants us to abandon our hearts, decisions, and plans to Him. Jesus never stops short, sending us sailing into oncoming traffic. We can trust Him to get us safely to our destination. Join me in praying for a large dose of child-like, handle-bar faith today.

"He called a little child to him, and placed the child among them. ³ And he said: 'Truly I tell you, unless you change and become like little children, you will never enter the kingdom of heaven. ⁴ Therefore, whoever takes the lowly position of this child is the greatest in the kingdom of heaven.'" Matthew 18:2-4

Delightful Welcome

A story of sweet hospitality!

Recently I had the pleasure of visiting my cousin for the afternoon. Upon my arrival, I knocked, the door was opened, and I was invited inside—all as usual. But this time I had barely stepped into the entry way when around the corner sprang the cutest, most joyful little girl—she was my cousin's two-year-old daughter. She was wearing her sweater dress, she had a big bow in her blonde hair, and chubby feet were bare. She wore the biggest and happiest smile—from ear to ear; her eyes were big and bright. She bounded right up to me and as she approached, she loudly and gleefully proclaimed, *"I'm so glad you came!"* She then snuggled close to my leg and I grabbed her up in my arms for a sweet embrace. It was the most delightful welcome—one filled with joyful sincerity. Her greeting held such warmth and invitation. My cousin and I looked at each other, surprised and tickled by her words. This precious child showed me loving hospitality. She was a faithful (little) steward of God's grace toward me as I entered her home that day. I'm tempted to begin greeting my guests this way. I can't imagine that anyone wouldn't enjoy such a loving reception. May we all, both offer and be surprised by such a delightful welcome.

"Offer hospitality to one another without grumbling. "[10] Each of you should use whatever gift you have received to serve others, as faithful stewards of God's grace in its various forms. "[11] If anyone speaks, they should do so as one who speaks the very words of God. If

26

anyone serves, they should do so with the strength God provides, so that in all things God may be praised through Jesus Christ. To him be the glory and the power for ever and ever. Amen." 1 Peter 4:9-11

Ever Faithful

Living in Southern California leaves a lot to be desired in the rain department. It seems we are often experiencing a drought. This particular morning though, I happened to glance out the kitchen window only to notice the rustling leaves and the clouds that had moved in to mix with the sunshine. I then observed that the patio was getting darker in spots as some droplets of rain fell. In my excitement, I yelled to my family and ran to look out the front door. I knew that if there was rain *and* sunshine there was bound to be a rainbow. Sure enough there was not only one, but two right outside my front door—a double rainbow! As I marveled at the glorious colors I was reminded of how ever-faithful our God is. His promises remain in effect for all of eternity. Whether we feel like we are parched in a season of drought, or drowning in the flood, God is with us. He continually pours out a double blessing on our lives as we lean on Him, look to Him, and follow Him.

What a wonderful way to start the morning, being reminded of God's faithfulness to me! And He is faithful to you.

"I have set my bow in the cloud, and it shall be a sign of the covenant

between me and the earth." Genesis 9:13

In the Waiting

When we realize that *everything* God does is good and perfect we will *want* to follow Him. While we perceive what is immediately in front of us, God foresees our whole life laid out before Him. The desires we have for ourselves are not always the best option. But God's plan is always the best option—He knows which paths we should take, and which ones we should stay far from. He divinely discerns which relationships will bless us, and which ones will hurt us. He perfectly forecasts the job where we will find fulfillment, and the one where we will not. He is aware and intimately acquainted with every detail of our lives. He knows the decisions we are faced with every day, and even every moment. And He offers His help.

Access to His help is found when we stop, pray, and listen for His voice. Often though, the last thing we want to do is stop, much less pause for an answer from God. We are in such a hurry, we try to rush God with His guidance, or try to push Him into answering per our will (which we can't). Following God requires faith and patience.

Though I sometimes secretly wish God would send me a note with exact instructions for my life, I know that would neither benefit my faith, nor increase my patience. These are both grown in times of surrender and waiting.

"Trust in the LORD with all your heart and lean not on your own understanding; in all your ways acknowledge Him, and He will make your paths straight." Proverbs 3:5-6

This Day

Each new day we have is a gift from God, waiting to be opened and appreciated. It's important to be intentional with how we use this gift. It is essential that we focus our attention on *here and now*, not worrying about tomorrow or fretting about the past. Worrying and fretting just steal the precious resource of time in the present.

"This is the day the LORD has made, let us rejoice and be glad in it."

Psalm 118:24 ESV

Scripture gives us countless guidelines for making the most of our time, but here are just three of the basics:

1- Rejoice in it—thoughtfully focus on making the most of *this day*, by rejoicing in it and the gift that it is. Even though life can be quite difficult, we can still find reason to celebrate, by remembering that God is good, He is faithful, and He is with us. With God, *this day* also holds the possibility of change, and the promise of hope.
2- Appreciate it—don't waste *this day*, this precious gift of time, by letting it slip away unused and unappreciated. We cannot get the time back once it has passed.
3- Invest in it—be careful and mindful of how we use and spend our time. As *this day* begins and we choose how to thoughtfully invest in it, we would be wise to consider these questions: Is this a good use of my day? Is it beneficial? Is this wise? Will this be a blessing to me or others, and does it honor God?

We never know what the next day holds, we only have the gift of today. So, let's accept it, open it, appreciate it, and use it to the fullest.

"Be careful then how you live, making the most of every opportunity." Ephesians 5:15-16

For Every Day

I believe there are two things of utmost importance *for every day* that we are given...

Be present in the moment.

Wear an attitude of love and grace.

"Dear friends, let us continue to love one another, for love comes from God." 1 John 4:7

Great and Small

God is intimately involved in the making of every one of His creations; every creature, both great and small are made with the loving care of the Father's hands. Long ago, God set the world in motion, and He has kept it spinning ever since. He is continually bringing fresh life to this planet, and He cares deeply about every new breath.

God knows when a bird falls out of its nest. He knows every hair on your head. He catches every tear drop that falls. No detail is too small for His attention. He created you, He loves you, and He constantly cares for you.

"Are not two sparrows sold for a penny? And not one of them will fall to the ground apart from your Father. [30] But even the hairs of your head are all numbered. [31] Fear not, therefore; you are of more value than many sparrows." Matthew 10:29-31

For Keeps

"'Martha, Martha,' the Lord answered, 'You are worried and upset about many things, but few things are needed—or indeed only one. Mary has chosen what is better, and it will not be taken away from her.'" Luke 10:41-42

There are many things that can worry and upset us—troubles, hardships, and like Martha, even busyness. I can so often identify with Martha and her misplaced focus. I fret about things that are good and important at that instance, but have no real lasting value. I can hear Jesus saying, "Tracy you are worried and upset about many things." Oh, to be instead like Mary, sitting at the feet of Jesus, soaking in His Presence, letting Him revitalize my soul. When I reprioritize, and make time with Jesus my number one priority, I am then able to tend to the things that demand my attention with a proper, more peaceful perspective.

Time with Jesus is always a wise investment, which holds eternal value. The treasures that come from these encounters will not be taken from us. They are for keeps.

Good Gifts to Share

God has equipped each of us with special talents, skills, and gifts. Every one of us has been blessed with wonderful and unique abilities. These blessings are meant not only for our personal enjoyment; they are to be used to bless others and honor God. And ultimately, that brings us great pleasure too. God is the giver of all our good gifts, and it is our honor to use them for His glory. So, take time this week to ask God to reveal to you any talent, skill, or gift He has given, that He would like you to start sharing with others. It could be as simple as calling someone God places on your heart, or helping a friend organize her home, or even taking someone a meal. Listening, helping, cooking—all useful abilities for blessing others.

"and I have filled him with the Spirit of God, with skill, ability and knowledge of all kinds of crafts." Exodus 31:3

"There are different kinds of gifts, but the same Spirit. There are different kinds of service, but the same LORD. There are different kinds of working, but the same God works all of them in all men."

1 Corinthians 12:4-6

Just Be

Find rest in God's Presence. Cease your endless striving and restlessness. Find rest in His care. All God asks of you is to *be*—be still, be content, be filled, be restored, be refreshed in His Presence and care.

"Yes, my soul, find rest in God; my hope comes from him."

Psalm 62:5

Half-Full

Opening our mouths in thanksgiving brings glory to God. By acknowledging our blessings as gifts from Him, He is praised.

"Every good and perfect gift is from above." James 1:15

Giving thanks also has the power to change our outlook. When we offer up gratitude to the Lord our *glass half-empty* view promptly flips to be *glass half-full*.

Even when it seems there isn't a reason to rejoice, if we look hard enough we will undoubtedly discover many things for which to be thankful. The perfect place to begin is by thanking God for His abundant love, and His salvation, mercy and grace. For the air in our lungs, and for the beauty of creation. We can thank Him for our health, and for doctors to care for us. Thank Him for the blessing of family, and friends.

Praise Him for the freedom in our nation to study His Word without fear, and for His assured promise that He is with us always. Thank Him for the hope of eternity.

As we thank our Father in Heaven we are reminded of His goodness to us. Giving thanks refreshes our weary spirits, and lightens our heavy hearts. Through words of gratitude we are strengthened with hope, courage, peace, and joy. Once praise and thanksgiving begin to flow from our lips, we quickly notice a joyful change in our heart.

"Enter his gates with thanksgiving and his courts with praise; give thanks to him and praise his name." Psalm 100:4

Heavenly Handiwork

Except for the quiet hum of a fan, I like to slumber in complete silence. My ears are often on over-active duty though, finely tuned in to hear every little sound, even when I'm sleeping. One night, at exactly 2:12 AM, I became aware of the soft padded paws of my dog rustling and wandering around at the foot of my bed. Ordinarily he sleeps in his comfy bed in the hallway. Years ago, he slept in our room, but that stopped when his snoring began. My dog is a beagle, which is a relative of the hound dog. So, it seems his overly-sensitive nose had gone into overtime. The scent of an animal passing by must have drifted in through my open bedroom window and out into the hall where it caught his attention, rousing him from sleep. Soon he was standing below my window inhaling very loudly. I went to calm him and put him back to bed, but then thought to take him outside for a quick break first. Knowing there may be coyotes nearby I put his leash on so he couldn't wander away from my side. I took him into the backyard and stood there waiting for him in the pitch-black night. I glanced up toward the sky to see the brilliance of a million twinkling lights above me. The sight was both awe-inspiring, and comforting. The sky was perfectly clear and the night was completely still, except for my dog and me. That night as I stood gazing at the stars I was reminded of the amazing truth that our God never sleeps. He is continually watching over and protecting us. He even leaves a million breath-taking nightlights on to remind us.

I consider it a blessing to have witnessed such an awesome part of creation that I usually sleep right through.

Thank You, God, for getting me out of bed to enjoy your heavenly handiwork, and for reminding me that I am safe in Your unfailing care. Amen.

"The heavens declare the glory of God; the sky displays his handiwork." Psalm 19:1

"I will lie down and sleep in peace, for you alone, O LORD, make me dwell in safety." Psalm 4:8

Honeysuckle Day

This morning as I took a morning walk before church I prayed, "Dear LORD, help me to notice the beauty all around me, lift my eyes and make me aware of all the sights, sounds and smells that surround me; help me to feel Your Presence, and live surrendered to You today. Help me to not be consumed by the menial tasks that demand my attention, but instead put You first, making You my number one priority, and letting all else fall into place. Thank You, LORD, for Your peace which surpasses all understanding. In Jesus' Name, Amen."

As I continued walking, I encountered the sweet fragrance of honeysuckle floating in the air. I leaned in close to the vine and cupping a blossom in my hands, I gently inhaled its intoxicating fragrance. With the aroma of honeysuckle still lingering in my mind, I became aware of the sweet fragrance of God's Presence in every detail of my day.

"But thanks be to God, who always leads us in triumph in Christ, and manifests through us the sweet aroma of the knowledge of Him in every place." 2 Corinthians 2:14

Clearing Clutter

Walking outside is my favorite form of exercise. I find that it not only keeps my body healthy, it carries amazing benefits for my mind and spirit as well. As I head outside—closing the front door behind, letting all responsibilities go for a while—my mind has a chance to clear out all the clutter of unnecessary things that start to bog it down and clog it up. It is a wonderful time to reassess the priorities of which things and tasks are of any importance. I am free to refocus onto things that are of true value. Most often my thoughts turn to God when I'm out enjoying His creation, which grants me great spiritual benefits—my inner being is revived in His Presence.

God is my favorite walking partner. He's a great listener; He offers great wisdom and advice, and He always walks at the perfect pace.

"I pray that out of his glorious riches he may strengthen you with power through his Spirit in your inner being," Ephesians 3:16

It Applies

All around my neighborhood are beautiful, majestic mountains. Sometimes I gaze at them with great joy, and occasionally it is with a heavy heart. Often as I walk, surrounded by these mountains, a song comes to mind which is based on the words found in Psalm 121:1-2, *"I lift my eyes up to the hills, where does my help come from? My help comes from the Lord, maker of heaven and earth."*

One day as I walked with God and I sang this song, I found that I could substitute all my blessings and life situations in place of the word "help." I sang, "Where does my *strength* come from?" "Where does my *health* come from?" "Where does my *family* come from?" "Where does my *salvation* come from?" "Where do my *friends* come from?" "Where does my *home* come from?" "Where do my *provisions* come from?" I sang, "Where do my *joy, hope, and peace* come from?"

It applies to everything! *Everything* I have comes from the LORD, Maker of Heaven and Earth. *Everything* that comes into my life must first pass through the loving hand of God.

There is no better way to come home refreshed from a walk than with this song in your heart and praise on your lips. There is comfort in knowing that everything comes from the LORD.

Dandelion Prayers

A silly excitement bubbles up inside me whenever I come across a Dandelion. To me it's a flower that represents hope. When I was a child, I made wishes on them, but through the years I have learned to make prayers on them. You see there is a big difference between wishes and prayers: wishes blow aimlessly in the wind, while our prayers are carried on the wings of angels into the throne room of God Almighty. Each time I hold a Dandelion between my fingers, I marvel at how something can be so simple, yet so wondrously complex at the same time. And as I reflect on the fact that God made this precious flower, I am filled with hope and confidence. I take a deep breath in, fill my cheeks with air, and blow out with a powerful whoosh. I then watch as the tiny, white, cottony puffs float effortlessly up toward the heavens, whisking my thanksgiving, cares, and prayers upward to God, who receives it all.

Excerpt from *"A Daughter of the King."*

"Each one had a harp and they were holding golden bowls full of incense, which are the prayers of God's people." Revelation 5:8

Belief

Do you ever want to believe so badly, only to have fear hold you back? Do you want to trust God for a miracle, but fear disappointment? Do you hope for a restored relationship, but fear forgiveness is too hard? Do you want to pray for healing, but out of fear resign yourself to the lie that it just can't happen for you? Fear is often the only thing standing in the way of our belief; It's a big obstacle—but, no obstacle is too large for God to overcome. With His help, we can conquer fear, and believe. We can even ask Him to help us with any trepidation and unbelief holding us back. He is faithful to deliver.

"Immediately the boy's father exclaimed, 'I do believe; help me overcome my unbelief!'" Mark 9:24

By handing our fear over to the Lord, we have freedom to move forward in belief.

Overcomer

As a child of God and a believer in Jesus Christ, we have the power to overcome difficulties and experience abundant life despite them. Jesus accomplished victory for us on the Cross of Calvary. We must daily choose to walk in this victory though. To maintain our triumphant position, we must consciously keep our eyes focused on Jesus.

"fixing our eyes on Jesus, the pioneer and perfecter of faith. For the joy set before him he endured the cross, scorning its shame, and sat down at the right hand of the throne of God." Hebrews 12:2

Refreshment

Whenever California is in a season of drought residents are asked to cut back on their water use in every possible way. As you drive the streets of our neighborhood, the cut in water use becomes evident rather quickly; the lawns which use to be lush and green, now have large brown, crunchy, dry spots. A brown lawn is now the badge of pride in the neighborhood, representing that you are you doing your part to conserve.

This morning I went out into the backyard to take in the cool fresh air before the heat overtook the day. As I stood there surveying the hills and sky around me, I felt the delightful sprinkle of tiny wet drops landing on my skin. It wasn't much in the way of precipitation, but I appreciated every little bit. I could hear the birds chirping, and if I listened hard enough I'm sure I would hear the parched hills exhaling a sigh of "ahhh" as they absorbed whatever moisture fell on them, providing a bit of necessary refreshment.

I can totally relate to the hills that have been deprived of some much-needed water. Just as the land needs constant watering to be its best— lush, green, vibrant, and growing strong— I need time alone with the Lord to be revived. To be my best, to feel vibrant and alive, and to keep growing in the right direction, I need time in God's Word; I need special, quiet time to talk with Him alone—just Him and me, heart to heart; I need time with girlfriends who share my love of the Lord, for we can encourage each other. I exhale a sigh of "ahhh" as these precious times water my very soul. Without these vital periods of refreshment, I quickly grow parched and my attitude can get *crunchy* like the dry brown lawn. Just like crunchy, brown grass is no fun to walk on, a crunchy brown attitude brings no pleasure to anyone.

It may be a good idea for me to get a hat to wear as a caution to others during my times with the Lord, but Instead of writing "Do Not Disturb" across the front, it would say "Soul Watering in Progress".

"But blessed is the one who trusts in the LORD, whose confidence is in him.[8] They will be like a tree planted by the water that sends out its roots by the stream. It does not fear when heat comes; its leaves are always green. It has no worries in a year of drought and never fails to bear fruit." Jeremiah 17:7-8

Rightfully Yours

Joy is a gift from God. It is an eternal blessing you are meant to keep. People and situations will come along and try to steal your joy. Like a bandana-masked train robber, they will interrupt your lovely ride, and with gun in hand forcefully command, "Stick 'em up, and give me all your joy." The joy rightfully belongs to you! You can share it with others, but don't let anyone take it from you.

"You have endowed him with eternal blessing and given him the joy of your presence." Psalm 21:6

No Secret

As the mother of two boys, I am sometimes asked what has most helped me throughout my parenting. I mention a few ideas, but always at the top of my list is *prayer*. Sometimes I get the response of a chuckle, like "No, what's the real secret?" Actually, it is not a secret at all. Prayer is available to all. Turning to God means I don't have to parent or do any aspect of life in my own strength or wisdom. I don't send up wishes that just get blown along in the wind; I offer up prayers to a real God, who hears me. I don't try to generate positive energy on my own; I ask God to guide and direct my path, and that of my sons too, and that is a truly positive thing! God is my ever-present help; He is my Comforter, Counselor, and Savior. He knows my life and the lives of my children better than I do. I seek His face to know His will for us, and then I aim to follow His lead. My goal is to teach my sons to seek God for themselves too. My priority for my family and myself is that we walk hand in hand with God; the rest falls in line after that.

"I have no greater joy than to know that my children walk in the Truth." 3 John 1:4

"Do not be anxious about anything, but in everything, by prayer and petition, with thanksgiving, present your requests to God." Philippians 4:6

Try Again

You know what is so wonderful? The same fresh start we feel every New Years' Day, God offers to us every day. So, if we mess up on our resolutions after just a couple of weeks, it doesn't mean we should give up and wait till the next January first to try again. Each day is a brand-new opportunity to improve ourselves (with God's help), get things done (with His strength), and have more joy (with His perspective).

"The faithful love of the LORD never ends! His mercies never cease.

Great is his faithfulness; his mercies begin afresh each morning."

Lamentations 3:22-23

Outwardly Good

At the end of each day I'd like to be able to crawl into bed with the peaceful knowledge that in some small way I made the world a better place for someone. I want to know that I have made a difference somehow. Having a positive impact doesn't have to be some grand event. I may not be able to travel around the world and stamp out all hunger and poverty and violence, but that doesn't mean I am powerless to make a difference in the lives of others. I can begin with something as simple as a smile to brighten someone's day. I can say an acknowledgement of "hello" to let someone know they matter enough to be noticed. I can offer a helping hand to someone in need of assistance. I can listen with a sympathetic ear, or speak a reassuring word of wisdom and comfort.

I pray that God would help me to not be so inwardly focused that I am not outwardly good to others. That He would give me eyes to see the opportunities to bless others right around me.

There are heavy hearts all around each of us in our everyday sphere of interaction. Hearts just waiting for someone to care and reach out.

"Let each of you look not only to his own interests, but also to the interests of others." Philippians 2:4

Thrive

As followers of Jesus we have the greatest hope of all. It is a hope that is ours from now into eternity. As we go about our daily life we encounter many ups and downs. Circumstances, situations, people, and things are constantly changing, bringing uncertainty. The one constant we can hold onto is the loving and unchanging character of God. He alone is the hope that will always prove faithful for us.

"But blessed is the man who trusts in the LORD, whose confidence is in Him. He will be like a tree planted by the water that sends out its roots by the stream, it does not fear when the heat comes; its leaves are always green. It has no worries in a year of drought and never fails to bear fruit." Jeremiah 17:7-8

From this scripture and our daily experience, we know that following Jesus does not exclude us from all trials or promise us a perfectly smooth life. It says that difficult times of heat and drought will continue to come upon us. But, as believers in Christ we have an amazing hope. As hard times inevitably come we don't faint or wither, but instead continue to grow, because we have the stream of life available to us. We need only look to the LORD to refresh, strengthen, and lead us through. As we face trials of various kinds we will continue to survive and even thrive as our roots go deep, and we trust in the LORD to sustain us.

Know Him

Jesus came to bring us salvation, and so much more. We often approach our faith for eternal salvation only, missing out on the countless other benefits and reasons that God sent His Son. The whole purpose of salvation was to restore what was broken—our relationship with God. Salvation came to break down barriers of sin and eternal death, but it also came to rebuild connections of love. Salvation built the bridge bringing us home to our Father; a Father who desperately wants us to know Him. He desires intimacy with us. He has given us His Own Spirit to bring revelation of who He truly is. He wants us to sincerely *know Him*, not just know *about* Him from afar.

"I keep asking that the God of our Lord Jesus Christ, the glorious Father, may give you the Spirit of wisdom and revelation, so that you may know him better." Ephesians 1:17

Redeemed

There is no sin God can't forgive, no life He can't transform, no story He can't use for His amazing glory.

What appears hopeless to us, has great possibility with God. He can and does forgive every sin imaginable as we accept Jesus Christ as our Lord and Savior. He wipes away our sin and gives us a new identity as His child. He redeems our weaknesses as we lean on Him, and He strengthens us to do things we never dreamed we could. God redeems our broken relationships; He can rescue a marriage from the brink of divorce, and heal a friendship of deep wounds. He brings new life to things we have long given up on. God redeems our seemingly meaningless trials and tribulations for His good purpose and our ultimate benefit; He uses them to draw us into His Presence for rest and refinement. Nothing is ever wasted.

Every sin, every choice and situation, every relationship, every loss grieved, every spoken word or action carried out, and every thought of worry, regret, bitterness, and hopelessness can be redeemed by the God of mercy and grace. God looks at our messy lives and sees beautiful potential in them. There is absolutely nothing in our lives (no matter how bad), that God cannot redeem and transform into something good, but first we must be willing to turn it over to Him, and allow Him to work His mighty miracles in our lives. God redeems the burnt-out ashes in our lives, turning them into a *crown of beauty and a garment of praise.* Our redeemed lives are a glorious *display of the LORD's splendor.*

"to proclaim the year of the LORD's favor and the day of

vengeance of our God, to comfort all who mourn,

³ and provide for those who grieve in Zion—

to bestow on them a crown of beauty instead of ashes,

the oil of joy instead of mourning, and a garment of praise instead

of a spirit of despair. They will be called oaks of righteousness, a

planting of the LORD for the display of his splendor.

⁴ They will rebuild the ancient ruins and restore the places long

devastated; they will renew the ruined cities that have been

devastated for generations." Isaiah 61:2-4

Respite for My Soul

As I sit here this morning, with the sun rising to take its place in the sky, I tune my ears to hear the chirps of the birds in the trees above me; I hear the buzzing of the bees in the bushes nearby; my eyes capture the slight swaying of the leaves on the trees as an almost undetectable breeze passes by. Some of the birds, with their bright red breasts have hopped down to nibble on seeds that have fallen to the ground. What a wonderful moment of solitude I find here, what a respite for my soul.

My life is very full, busy, and active, just like most people. But, for me to function at my best in each of the activities on my plate, I must also make time to recharge my mind and soul.

Without these precious moments stolen away for my well-being, I would start to run on empty, and begin to sputter and stall. Just like a car, I've got to refuel, and once refueled I can get back on the busy road and find enjoyment in that too. I find that quiet times in my garden, before the day begins, are like the service station for my soul— Fill 'er up, and send me on my way!

"God, my shepherd! I don't need a thing. You have bedded me down in lush meadows, you find me quiet pools to drink from. True to Your Word, you let me catch my breath and send me in the right direction." Psalm 23

Very Good

When God made the birds and fish, He said, "It is good." When He made the animals of the land, He said, "It is good." When he placed the stars, moon, and sun in the heavens, He said, "It is good." When He made you, a smile of great pleasure spread across His face, and He said, "It is very good." God doesn't make mistakes. He made you just the way you are, special and unique, unlike anyone else. Let God's words sink into your heart and mind and give you the encouragement and confidence to be uniquely YOU today.

Excerpt from *"A Daughter of the King."*

"God saw all that he had made, and it was very good." Genesis 1:31

Rose Smeller

Through the years my Dad has passed down more than a few qualities to me. My Dad has always possessed a great appreciation for the beauty of nature. He is an artist by profession, but it is his personal art which best portrays and captures this appreciation; he paints, he sketches he photographs. His art captures the majesty of creation at its best—the sky with its varying colors on display, the clouds floating effortlessly by, the sea with its changing emotions of gentleness and power, the desert landscapes both serene and harsh at the same time. With the eye of an artist he sees the big picture and notices the tiniest detail. He is the one who taught me to stop and smell the roses.

When I was a young girl the neighbors across the street from my grandparents had a yard brimming with rose bushes. Every color imaginable filled their front yard. One afternoon my Dad took me across to their garden and photographed me standing amongst the blooms. He snapped some of me admiring the roses, and some of me leaning in to smell them. In this way, he truly did hand down his appreciation of roses, and all flowers for that matter.

Another trait my Dad passed down to me is his very fast walking pace. As a little girl, with little legs, I would do my best to keep up with him. Because of this training I'm a fast walker even now, but nonetheless I still take time to stop and smell the roses. I walk around the block almost every day, and as I approach yards with roses out front, I purposefully bring my feet to a halt, lean in, and deeply inhale the fragrance of the bloom. The sweetness brings me to my senses, helping me appreciate my surroundings.

Let's face it, life is not always full of roses, so when we do encounter them along the way we need to be sure to enjoy them.

"Look, the winter is past, and the rains are over and gone. The flowers are springing up, the season of singing birds has come,"

Song of Solomon 2:11-12

In the fast pace of everyday life, we must purposefully pause and take in our surroundings. Be mindful of the beauty you encounter today, and take time to stop and smell the roses.

Side by Side

We are never too old for fun and adventure, and what a joy when we find someone to join us in doing something very spontaneous and out of the ordinary! For some strange reason, since we moved into our house I have wanted to sleep out on our balcony. And until recently, I had not been able to find anyone to join me—imagine that! My always adventurous sister was staying over one night and as we stood in the backyard looking up at the stars I mentioned my desire to sleep on the balcony (in the front of the house), and to my surprise she immediately *volunteered* to join me that very night. I was filled with giddiness and glee! I excitedly ran to find the sleeping bags and pillows, and a couple of thick blankets to cushion the floor. We quickly got our pajamas on, went out onto the balcony, and climbed into our sleeping bags. We lay there like kids, side by side in the dark; talking heart to heart, giggling like young girls, while staring at the Big Dipper which spread out in the sky before our very eyes. We heard the crickets chirping and the frogs croaking; a fountain trickled in the distance; random dogs let out a bark now and then, and a cool breeze gently blew past, barely brushing over our faces.

Two adult women, both sisters and friends, choosing to sleep on a balcony when two perfectly comfy beds awaited inside. Was what we did practical? Was it well-planned out? Was it even considered normal? Absolutely not! And that's what made it so much fun! I thank the LORD for the joy that is found in the spontaneous, out of the ordinary things, and I thank the LORD even more, for my sister who was by my side in this whacky adventure. It was perfect that after all these years, she was the one who camped out, side by side with me.

"Two are better than one because they have a good return for their labor. For if either of them falls, the one will lift up his companion. But woe to the one who falls when there is not another to lift him up. Furthermore, if two lie down together they keep warm, but how can one be warm *alone*? And if one can overpower him who is alone, two can resist him. A cord of three *strands* is not quickly torn apart." Ecclesiastes 4:9-12

Priceless

Somethings you just can't put a price on—they are *priceless*. Nothing is more appropriately called *priceless* than the Kingdom of Heaven. Entrance into God's Kingdom cannot be bought or earned by the hands of man—the price is too high. Very fortunately our entry into the Kingdom was purchased by the sacrifice of Jesus—He gave His life, so we could reside with Him forever. The Kingdom of Heaven is so resplendent and awesome, that if needed, we would willingly sell everything we own, going into debt even, just for a glimpse of its glory. But thanks be to our LORD and Savior for His amazing gift, the treasure of Heaven is ours to keep.

"The kingdom of heaven is like treasure hidden in a field. When a man found it, he hid it again, and then in his joy went and sold all he had and bought that field." Matthew 13:44

Three Things

"He has showed you, O man, what is good. And what does the

LORD require of you? To act justly, and to love mercy, and to walk

humbly with your God." Micah 6:8

Being that we humans tend to complicate things, God has simplified matters by providing us with a list of three things He requires.

1- *To act justly*—this purely means we live by God's standard, His way, and His righteousness. He's even graciously given us an instruction manual for further guidance—it's the Bible.

2- *To love mercy*—this simply means to show favor to others; to offer kindness and goodness toward others as the LORD has shown us. It means we see them through eyes of compassion and understanding, no matter who they are or what they've done.

3- *To walk humbly with your God*—the third on the list requires that we surrender control, follow God's lead, and trust that His ways are better than our own. He is God after all, and we are not.

He requires justice, love, and humility—three worthy goals to live by.

Tiny Pops

Venturing around the block this morning I noticed a yard that was alive with tiny purple flowers poking out from between the green blades of grass. Continuing along the path at the neighborhood park I was greeted by sunny pops of bright yellow, as dandelions sprouted out cheerily amongst the grass. I also noticed little pops of white clover blossoms popping out to make their appearance. These tiny pops of color brought a smile to my face. Most people view these colorful surprises as intrusive invaders and work hard to keep them out of their otherwise perfect yard. They pursue the conception of a perfectly manicured lawn.

It's kind of how life is (at least mine). I get a vision—I have a plan—of how things should go. And I get overwhelmed when the unexpected pops up, when there is a so-called invader in my otherwise smooth plans. I thank God for this reminder, that when I try to control things too tightly and keep everything perfectly manicured there leaves little to no room for Him to put tiny, unexpected, beautiful pops of color into my life, or even my day. I pray that I leave room for the tiny pops of purple, yellow, and white flowers from God to grow in my life.

"Many, LORD my God, are the wonders you have done, the things you planned for us. None can compare with you; were I to speak and tell of your deeds, they would be too many to declare." Psalm 40:5

Untangled

On my own:

I am insecure.

I am awkward.

I am broken.

On my own I am a jumbled mess of feelings, most of which are built on lies meant to keep me from living the abundant life God has for me.

With Jesus:

I am secure.

I am confident.

I am mended.

I am whole.

With Jesus, I am untangled and set free. With Jesus, I learn the Truth of who I am.

With Jesus, I find abundance:

I find love.

I find joy.

I find acceptance.

I find peace.

I find security.

With Jesus, I am untangled.

Such Things

There is a lot of nonsense that tries to take up residence in our minds. Too often we focus on thoughts of worry, fear, shame, regret, bitterness, hatred, envy, and pride. We not only allow these thoughts to be there, we offer them an open door and invite them to stay. They gain what the Bible refers to as a *foothold*. We play certain thoughts over and over in our minds like a broken record, getting stuck in an awful groove. Well, it's time to pick up the needle and play a new song. God has made us a new playlist of some lovely thoughts, and He recommends we listen to them often. He tells us to think on excellent things that are worthy of praise; to turn off the nonsense and listen to truth—His Truth. Think about such things as these.

"Finally, brothers and sisters, whatever is true, whatever is noble, whatever is right, whatever is pure, whatever is lovely, whatever is admirable—if anything is excellent or praiseworthy—think about such things." Philippians 4:8

Beautiful Variety

Whenever I sit in my backyard, surrounded by beautiful flowers, I am reminded of each of the lovely women in my life. As my gaze wanders around the yard my eyes land on the flowers one by one; each is unique and beautiful in its own special way.

There are the robust, pink ones, full and bright; the petite, cheery, orange tinted ones; the white, delicate blooms; the tight yellow buds still waiting to blossom. There is a pale lavender one hiding amidst them all. Each flower has its own color, shape, size, and fragrance. God in His creative sovereignty made them each uniquely different, but all equally beautiful. My hope is that every dear woman, some I know, others I may never meet, would come to celebrate her own beauty, to realize her own worth just as she is, not comparing herself to the woman next to her. I hope that she loves and accepts herself just the way she has been created. I am so glad that God has put a variety of flowers in my yard, and I am so very glad that He has put a wide variety of women in my life. Each is a beautiful blessing to me in her own special way.

Excerpt from *"A Daughter of the King."*

"He has made everything beautiful in its time. He has also set eternity in the human heart; yet no one can fathom what God has done from beginning to end." Ecclesiastes 3:11

Strength

When times get tough we often try to muster strength from within ourselves to get through the situation, yet we quickly become aware of our own insufficiency, and grow tired under the weight of carrying the load alone.

We may then turn to others for strength, hoping their boost of muscle will carry us through. This may be good in the short-term, but their muscles will ultimately grow tired over time too.

What we need is the mighty power of Jesus. His strength never falters, never weakens, and never fails. The strength of Jesus never tires. Ask Him to come alongside you and lift the burden from your shoulders. You were never meant to carry it alone.

"but those who hope in the LORD will renew their strength. They will soar on wings like eagles; they will run and not grow weary, they will walk and not be faint." Isaiah 40:31

Bless Your Heart

A famous phrase of my Grandma's was, "Bless her or his heart," depending on whom she was speaking of. It was her term of endearment, her words of adoration for the ones she held dear. My Grandma loved the Lord dearly, and she loved His children too. She is the one who shared with me this love and shepherded me to find it for myself as well. Her words hold such beauty and warmth—what more could we ask than for God to bless someone's heart? Our hearts hold the key to our being. It is where we truly feel, experience, and embrace life. Hearts are fragile and can easily be broken. Hearts need constant care and nurturing. Hearts sometimes require healing and mending. Hearts can inspire us beyond belief.

Our hearts need God's continual blessing, so right now I say to you, "Bless your heart."

"Delight yourself in the LORD, and he will give you the desires of your heart." Psalm 37:4 ESV

Highest Honor

God has bestowed on you the greatest responsibility—being an ambassador for His Heavenly Kingdom. He has endowed you with the royal position of representing Jesus to the world, by sharing His Message of love, mercy, grace, and reconciliation, which you have already experienced yourself.

As God's child, you are made worthy of this highest honor.

"We are therefore Christ's ambassadors, as though God were making his appeal through us. We implore you on Christ's behalf: Be reconciled to God." 2 Corinthians 5:20

Abandoned Heart

There is nothing more beautiful than a heart that has been fully surrendered and abandoned to God. This morning as I stood singing along with the worship band and the rest of the congregation at church, I noticed down in the very front row, standing alone, was a young girl about 7 years of age. She was singing praises to the LORD with her little arms fully outstretched, unaware of the adoring glances of others all around her. Her full abandonment to the moment and to the LORD was the most precious sight.

We sang, "I'll stand with arms high and heart abandoned, in awe of the One who gave it all; I'll stand, my soul LORD to you surrendered. All I am is yours." As we proclaimed this anthem, one by one, the arms of others sprang up around the room to join this little girl in surrender to the Savior. The room was filled with abandoned hearts—hearts overwhelmed by the Presence of the LORD, hearts full of worship and rejoicing, and hearts in the humble posture of surrender, with arms held high. Hearts trusting completely in His holy name.

"In him our hearts rejoice, for we trust in his holy name." Psalm 33:21

God wants your heart. God wants your praise and worship. He wants you. All of you.

Song by Michael W. Smith; Songwriters, Popper, John C.

Published by, Lyrics © Universal Music Publishing Group

Focus

It's all about our focus. We can't let ourselves get so caught up in the kingdom of Earth, that we lose focus of the Kingdom of Heaven. The Kingdom of Heaven holds eternal value—it is where our true hope lies.

"those who use the things of the world, as if not engrossed in them.

For this world in its present form is passing away." 1 Corinthians 7:31

Surpassing Love

There is nothing like love to make our minds race, and make our hearts soar. The power of love brings strength and resolve; it propels us forward with passion and zeal. There is no greater prayer than to ask for complete revelation of God's rich love—for our hearts to more fully grasp the lavish love that He has for us. His love makes all the difference. His surpassing love strengthens our inner being; the very depths of our soul are refreshed and invigorated as we come to more fully understand just how much He loves us. When we comprehend His limitless love, we are filled with the fullness of Him.

"I pray that out of his glorious riches he may strengthen you with power through his Spirit in your inner being, [17] so that Christ may dwell in your hearts through faith. And I pray that you, being rooted and established in love, [18] may have power, together with all the Lord's holy people, to grasp how wide and long and high and deep is the love of Christ, [19] and to know this love that surpasses knowledge—that you may be filled to the measure of all the fullness of God." Ephesians 3:16-19

Contentment

So often the pursuit of perfection—the perfect family, perfect job, perfect house, the perfect *me*, the perfect life—keeps us from enjoying what we have here and now. The thought that we will finally be happy *someday*, and *when we get there, or when we have that*, steal the satisfaction that could be ours right now. Joy, peace, and contentment are found by relishing and celebrating our current blessings.

"But godliness with contentment is great gain." 1 Timothy 6:6

In Step

Living by the Spirit, the very Spirit of God, brings noticeable change to our lives. Keeping in step with the Spirit, God's very own Spirit, yields glorious fruit as we walk with Him day by day, moment by moment. As He nourishes our hearts with His love, as He feeds our souls with joy and peace, and He waters our minds with His perspective, we can't help but bear fruit resembling His nature. As we live and keep in step with the Spirit of God, all His extraordinary attributes begin to take root in us, eventually growing into a beautiful display of His work in our lives. God is love, God is joy and peace, He is patient, kind, good and faithful. He is daily changing us to be more like Him.

"But the fruit of the Spirit is love, joy, peace, forbearance, kindness, goodness, faithfulness, ²³ gentleness and self-control. Against such things there is no law. ²⁴ Those who belong to Christ Jesus have crucified the flesh with its passions and desires. ²⁵ Since we live by the Spirit, let us keep in step with the Spirit." Galatians 5:22-25

Wonder-filled

There we stood gazing upward into the deep blue darkness of night. My Grandma had escorted me out to the front yard to share her appreciation for the sparkly wonders which filled the sky. She knowledgably pointed out the various constellations which had taken their assigned positions up above our heads. In reverence of the spectacle, she spoke in gentle whispers as she helped me discover the Big and Little Dippers. She drew my attention to the form of the ladle, showing me how the stars arranged perfectly to include a scooper and a handle. To this day I continue to search for the duo of Dippers. And as I do I remember my Grandma, but I also contemplate the amazing creativity and power of our Heavenly Father; the Creator of Heaven and Earth, and the moon and the stars. When I reflect on God's magnificent creation I am wonder-filled.

"Lift up your eyes and look to the heavens: Who created all these? He who brings out the starry host one by one and calls forth each of them by name. Because of his great power and mighty strength, not one of them is missing." Isaiah 40:26

Healing

Rather than nurse our wounds, letting them consume us, let's instead embrace the healing power available to us through Jesus, our loving Healer. Let's allow Him to bandage up the pain in our hearts as we turn our thoughts to the amazing sacrifice He made on our behalf—a sacrifice motivated by love. He asks us to bring our hurts to Him and exchange our wounds for His healing.

"But he was pierced for our transgressions, he was crushed for our iniquities; the punishment that brought us peace was on him, and by his wounds we are healed." Isaiah 53:3

The Trade

In order to receive the new, the fresh, the good, the best, we must be willing to surrender (give up, release) something in exchange.

Gifts such as love, joy, peace, hope, healing, confidence, forgiveness, freedom, and rest are waiting to be opened. These and more are available for us to grab up and envelop in our arms. There is one catch. We must let go of the old—the shame, regret, bitterness, unforgiveness, worry, fear—to make room for these new glorious gifts. It's time to lay down the stuff that's dragging us down. It's time to make an exchange—trade our heavy burdens for the easy burdens found at the Cross.

In Matthew 11:28-30, Jesus said, "'Come to me, all you who are weary and burdened, and I will give you rest. Take my yoke upon you and learn from me, for I am gentle and humble in heart, and you will find rest for your souls. For my yoke is easy and my burden is light.'"

Blessed Time

Truth be told, we cannot do it all. And we were never meant to. There are only so many hours in a day, and no matter how hard we try stretching time by cramming in as much as possible, the only thing that usually gets stretched is us—our patience, our energy, our joy. The miraculous key to expanding time is in using it wisely—not by making more hours in the day, but by being more choosey about our commitments. Before we sign up to lead one more committee, join one more group, organize one more activity, or even volunteer to help one more person, we need to assess our already over-loaded calendars. All of these *one mores* quickly add up to more than we can handle. Assessment comes by asking ourselves some good questions—*Do I have room for something new on my calendar? Is it time to discontinue, step down, or take a break from an activity I've been doing, to make room for something new that I'd rather be doing?* Just because we've always done something in the past doesn't mean we have to stick with it till we die.

Just as releasing our old burdens to the LORD leaves room for Him to pour out new blessings into our lives, we must often be willing to release some old commitments in order to receive the new ones He has for us. Loosening our grip of the calendar, and removing its hold over us, opens the door for new opportunities, new adventures, new experiences, new possibilities, and new blessings.

Time used properly is a blessing to be enjoyed, not a burden to be dreaded.

"There is a time for everything, and a season for every activity under the heavens..." Ecclesiastes 3:1

Able

When facing overwhelming challenges or obstacles it's best if we take our eyes off ourselves and our own ability, and instead focus on God and His ability. He is more than able to deliver us.

"If we are thrown into the blazing furnace, the God we serve is able to deliver us from it, and he will deliver us from Your Majesty's hand." Daniel 3:17

By Name

Every Saturday the local theater would hold afternoon matinees, which treated the neighborhood kids to two full-length children's movies, with a cartoon shown in-between. A drawing was also held between showings, when items such as bikes, games, and various toys were raffled off. You could feel the excitement of the audience grow as the lights went on and the announcer took the stage. We sat in eager anticipation at the thought of our name being called. On more than one occasion my dream came true. Sitting beside my friends I heard my name ring out over the loud speakers. I quickly sprang from my seat and made my way down the aisle. My eyes were focused on the stage, but I was well aware of the stares of my fellow attendees locked firmly on me. As happy as they were for me, everyone in that room would have loved to have been in my shoes. There are few experiences as joy-inducing as hearing our name called in recognition and for reward. We all desire acknowledgment and we all enjoy prizes.

I have news for you—a day is coming when God will invite you forward from among the crowd. He will call you by name and the words "well done my good and faithful servant" will flow from His mouth. He will award you the crown of His glory. He will bestow on you the blessings of eternal life.

"The one who is victorious will, like them, be dressed in white. I will never blot out the name of that person from the book of life, but will acknowledge that name before my Father and his angels."

Revelation 3:5

Power of Love

The love of God makes us conquerors in more ways than we can even count—His love saves, His love heals, His love guides and admonishes, His love refreshes and comforts, His love protects and strengthens... Whenever we feel weak or powerless we need only reflect on the sacrificial love that the Father has lavished on us.

Excerpt from, *"A Daughter of the King."*

"We are more than conquerors through Him who loved us."

Romans 8:37

Bubble Gum Compassions

As a child, Saturday outings with my Dad often included an afternoon at the park or a trip to the ice cream shop. One such occasion called for a serving of my usual favorite—a cone with double scoops of pink bubble gum, ice-creamy deliciousness. This treat was not only satisfying to my taste buds; it was pretty to look at. It was my favorite color—light pink—and it was filled with brightly colored balls of chewy bubble gum. So, when I finished my ice cream I always had the pleasure of bubble blowing to look forward to. Well, this one afternoon I had just received my wonderful treat, taken a lick or two, and as we exited the store my two scoops tumbled to the ground. As I witnessed my ice cream drop, my joy did too. My Dad quickly jumped into action on my behalf—he brought me back into the store and bought me a brand-new treat. He could have scolded me for wasting money and not being more careful; he could have said, "too bad," and let me watch as he continued enjoying his own ice cream cone—but he did none of this. He instead offered me grace and consolation, over my spilled ice cream cone. This is the same manner in which our Heavenly Father treats us. He doesn't say, "Too bad," or "You're out of luck," when we mess up either. He lovingly comes alongside and gives us another chance. He restores our joy with His understanding and grace. He offers endless bubble gum compassions.

"Because of the LORD's great love we are not consumed, for his compassions never fail. [23] They are new every morning; great is your faithfulness." Lamentations 3:22-23

Legacy

Faith is not something we accidentally pass on; faith is a legacy we purposefully choose to hand on to the next generation. Faith is kept alive as we share stories of God's holiness, love, faithfulness, and power shown throughout history to His people. Faith is shared, grown, and passed on as we unashamedly tell of His personal influence in our own lives.

"He decreed statutes for Jacob and established the law in Israel, which he commanded our ancestors to teach their children, ⁶ so the next generation would know them, even the children yet to be born, and they in turn would tell their children. ⁷ Then they would put their trust in God and would not forget his deeds but would keep his commands." Psalm 78:5-7

Our Story

"Give thanks to the LORD, for he is good;

his love endures forever.

² Let the redeemed of the LORD tell their story—

those he redeemed from the hand of the foe,

³ those he gathered from the lands,

from east and west, from north and south." Psalm 107:1-3

As God's redeemed, what are we so thankful for? What exactly is our story? That the LORD has purchased us back from the hand of our enemy, bringing us near to Himself. We give thanks that He took us from our wandering ways, and gave our weary hearts a place to rest.

With gratitude, we proclaim how He continually delivers us from our distresses, and offers us peace and hope amidst our trials. We rejoice as He leads us in the way of His perfect plan for our lives. We speak of the satisfaction found as He fills our searching souls with His over-flowing love. The redeemed of the LORD speak of His blessings with mouths of reverence and praise. As the redeemed of the LORD, we simply tell the story of God at work in our lives.

Each one of us who has been redeemed by God becomes a poster child of His goodness, love, and power through Jesus Christ. As His child, we each have sin that has been forgiven, we each have a life that's been transformed, and we each have a story to tell. A story that brings glory to the King of Mercy and Grace.

Your Authority

Dear Heavenly Father,

I am so grateful for Your loving-care. You alone are sovereign over all. Everything that happens in Heaven and on Earth is under Your authority. No matter how far this world seems to spin out of control, You remain in control. In You, I find peace, hope, and joy. My confidence is found in You alone. You are good, merciful, powerful, righteous, and just. Your ways prevail. Help me to keep focused on You. Amen.

"Yours, LORD, is the greatness and the power and the glory and the majesty and the splendor, for everything in heaven and earth is yours. Yours, LORD, is the kingdom; you are exalted as head over all. [12] Wealth and honor come from you; you are the ruler of all things. In your hands are strength and power to exalt and give strength to all." 1 Chronicles 29:11-12

Choice Words

Words hold great power— the power to bless and encourage, the power to hurt and tear down. Choosing our words wisely can prevent untold damage. Choosing our words wisely can reap immeasurable benefits. We can bring glory to our LORD with our mouths, or we can bring shame on ourselves with our tongues. Fortunately, God gives us many helpful guidelines on the proper use of our verbal skills.

1. Think before we speak.
2. Learn to hold our tongue. Not every thought that passes through our minds needs to spoke; not every opinion we hold needs to be shared.
3. Discern what is true and appropriate before speaking.
4. Fill our heart and mind with good things, because what we put in will ultimately spill out of our mouths.
5. Too many words give sin an opportunity to interject into the conversation. (gossiping, boasting, foolishness)
6. Use our words always for good, and never for evil.
7. Use words to bless others and to praise the LORD.
8. Use our words to speak life, hope, joy, and love.

"May these words of my mouth and this meditation of my heart be pleasing in your sight, LORD, my Rock and my Redeemer."

Psalm 19:14

A New List

Go here, go there. Do this, do that. Buy for him, buy for her. Make those lists and check them all twice. With all the hustle and bustle that usually comes with the Christmas season we often lose sight of what matters. We are often overcome with anxiety and hurriedness, instead of experiencing the peace and joy that Jesus came to give at this miraculous and holy time of year. At that first Christmas, so long ago in a stable full of curious animals, Mary and Joseph had their minds filled with a singular focus—the birth of their sweet baby Jesus. The shepherds who watched over the flocks by night heard the angels declare with joyous song, the arrival of The Son of God, The Savior of the world. Filled with awe and wonder they hurriedly ran to join the celebration in Bethlehem. Everything centered around the birth of Jesus on this most special night in all of history.

It is time to make a new list, and put Jesus first. Remember the simplicity of His beautiful and humble birth. Appreciate the grace and mercy that God has shown through the sacrifice of His only begotten Son. In His honor, let's love, give, and show kindness to others. Give smiles, hugs, and encouraging words freely in celebration of Him. Slow down and appreciate time with loved ones. Make memories. Bless others. A wondrously simple, yet brilliant new list.

"And there were shepherds living out in the fields nearby, keeping watch over their flocks at night. ⁹ An angel of the Lord appeared to them, and the glory of the Lord shone around them, and they were terrified. ¹⁰ But the angel said to them, 'Do not be afraid. I bring you good news that will cause great joy for all the people. "Today in the town of David a Savior has been born to you; he is the Messiah, the Lord. ¹²This will be a sign to you: You will find a baby wrapped in cloths and lying in a manger.'" Luke 2:8-12

J.O.Y.S.

For years, my Grandma and Grandpa ran a seasonal Christmas store at the local mall. A few of their kids (our parents) and some of us grandkids took turns helping. We would sort through and unpack boxes filled with Christmas goodies. We would delicately place ornaments among the branches and boughs of evergreen trees, and set up old-fashioned Christmas villages reminiscent of times gone by. It was a job, but it felt more like play. There was joy everywhere you turned. Nativity scenes showcasing the true meaning of Christmas were displayed all around. The birth of our Savior deserves a celebration and this store was brimming full. The name of the store was Christmas J.O.Y.S., which my Grandma explained stands for Jesus, others, and yourself. In what has turned into a season of *gimme, gimme, gimme*, my Grandparents store name stands as a reminder of the true spirit of the season— Jesus first, then others, and then yourself.

Beginning with the very first Christmas gift, when God gave His Own Son for the salvation of the world, the meaning of Christmas remains rooted in God's love. And His love lives on in our relationship with Jesus, and through our sharing, giving, and sacrificing for others. In this way, we best honor the birth of our Savior—loving Jesus, and loving others.

Let's give gifts to one another in a spirit of thanks, in honor of the Gift God gave for us.

"Thanks be to God for his indescribable gift!" 2 Corinthians 9:15

Cupcakes and Toothbrushes

Thinking back to a recent Christmas, one of my favorite memories is of spending time with my sons on Christmas Eve morning. Family was coming over for dinner, gifts, and all the usual festivities later that evening. We had ordered tamales for our meal so there wasn't much prep work needed, which freed us up for the morning. In the days leading up to Christmas I had decided to make some chocolate peppermint cupcakes, complete with sprinkles, to give as gifts. We usually give gifts to people we know—family, friends, neighbors, co-workers—but this year I had the idea to hand them out to the homeless people we regularly see at various locations around town. I figured they probably don't get many gifts, if any at all. I thought they would probably like a little care package as well. So along with the cupcakes, each person would receive a gift bag filled with toiletries, tied up with a Christmas bow. I was over-joyed that my sons were up for the adventure and wanted to join me. We drove around town on a Christmas Eve mission determined to give out these treats and share the love of Jesus. Each person we met was filled with gratitude, and touched by the fact that someone had thought of them. One man greeted us with a jovial "Merry Christmas." He was very kind and immediately ate his cupcake with gusto. Another man we met couldn't believe that we were doing this together as a family. As he sat on the street corner he made hand-drawn Christmas cards to share with people who passed by. We were fortunate to receive one. We had a short visit with most of the people we met. The one man we didn't get to visit with was asleep under a tree, by the side of the road. In this instance, we decided to let him sleep and my older son just set his goodies beside him. That didn't exactly go as planned— the man peeked one eye open and suddenly jumped up. I don't know who was more startled, him or my son. My son smiled, motioned to the cupcake and bag he had left, and then hurried back to the car. As we drove away the man was sitting upright under the tree, enjoying his cupcake. This encounter makes me smile just thinking of it. I think this might become a tradition. Cupcakes and toothbrushes represent the reciprocal gift of giving. As much as we give to others, through their joy they are giving to us in return.

"Defend the weak and the fatherless; uphold the cause of the

poor and the oppressed." Psalm 82:3

Lilies and Lemonade

Joy-filled Devotions, by You

(Space for you to write your prayers, thoughts, notes, and even your own joy-filled stories and devotions)

Lilies and Lemonade

Joy-filled Devotions, by You

Lilies and Lemonade

Joy-filled Devotions, by You

Lilies and Lemonade

Joy-filled Devotions, by You

Lilies and Lemonade

Joy-filled Devotions, by You

Lilies and Lemonade

Joy-filled Devotions, by You

Lilies and Lemonade

Joy-filled Devotions, by You

Lilies and Lemonade

Joy-filled Devotions, by You

Lilies and Lemonade

Joy-filled Devotions, by You

Lilies and Lemonade

Joy-filled Devotions, by You

Lilies and Lemonade

Joy-filled Devotions, by You

Lilies and Lemonade

Joy-filled Devotions, by You

Heartfelt Thanks

To Aunt Linda, for encouraging me to write.

To Camden, for a beautiful book cover, once again.

To Carolyn, for your dear friendship and words of
encouragement.

Eternal gratitude to Jesus, for filling my life with joy.

Getting to Know the Author

First and foremost, I am a woman who loves the Lord with all her heart. I am married to a wonderful man, and I'm a mother of two young men (who used to be small). I am a daughter, a sister, a friend, a neighbor. I have a dog, I enjoy taking walks outside, and I like chips and salsa. I serve in the women's ministry at my local church in Westlake Village, California. I enjoy speaking at Teen Challenge, and other various women's events. I have a passion for helping women deepen their relationship with Jesus and discover their identity as a child of God through the study of His Word. Although you and I may have different likes or dislikes, relationships or roles, I'm sure many of my life stories can be related to whatever you have going on. I truly thank you for joining me on this journey and hope that you find some encouragement as we walk together with the Lord.

My titles available in stores and on Amazon.com:

A Daughter of the King: Gaining Confidence as a Child of God

Lilies and Lemonade: Joy-Filled Devotions

Promise and Possibilities: Hope-Filled Devotions

Connect with me on Facebook at: facebook.com/tracyhillauthor

Follow my blog at: tracy-considerthelilies.blogspot.com

Made in the USA
Columbia, SC
16 June 2018